GW00363930

A Taste of Heligan
the best from the bakery

TINA BISHOP and PAUL DRYE

TRURAN

First published in 2003 by Truran, Croft Prince, Mount Hawke, Truro, Cornwall TR4 8EE
www.truranbooks.co.uk

Truran is an imprint of Truran Books Ltd

ISBN 1 85022 177 4 (p/b)
ISBN 1 85022 184 7 (h/b)

Text © Heligan Gardens Ltd
Illustrations © Sue Lewington

Printed and bound in Cornwall by
R. Booth Ltd, Antron Hill, Mabe, Penryn, Cornwall TR10 9HH

Paul would like to thank his wife Angela, for her love, enthusiasm and much typing, and past kitchen colleagues: Brenda, Joan, Pauline and Roger for their hard work, dedication, fun, laughter and friendship.

Tina would like to thank her Mum, Dad and her brother Robert, for their never-ending love and support, her sister Julie for her endless help and her husband Andrew for collating, interpreting and typing all her recipes – even if he did consume vast quantities of her chocolate cake in so doing!

Thanks must go to the entire catering team at Heligan for their good humour and hard work. A special mention goes to Kieron, Jeanette, Carol, Sue, Katy, Mary, Duncan, Simon, Jenny and Heather. Thanks also go to the gardening team: particularly Tom, Katharine, Charles and Clive. Thanks also to Julian 'snappy' Stephens for the author photograph and Candy Smit for her continuing enthusiasm and support.

The Willows Tearoom/Restaurant is open to non-garden visitors throughout the year from 10am daily, closing half an hour before the gardens.
For information about our summer Friday Feast Nights and for bookings, tel 01726 845100

The gardens are open all year round from 10 am daily.
The Lost Gardens of Heligan, Pentewan, St Austell, Cornwall PL26 6EN
Tel: 01726 845100   www.heligan.com

Introduction

Tina Bishop (Baker) and Paul Drye (Head Chef and Catering Manager)

We would like to welcome you to our collection of bread and cake recipes. Paul Drye (Head Chef and Catering Manager) spent his first year at Heligan developing and improving the bakery section before handing the baton over to Tina Bishop (Baker), who has gone on to increase the range of products while maintaining extremely high standards. Most noticeable recently is that the volume of production has been increasing, to such an extent that a new bakery has been built to accommodate this growing phenomenon.

Yes, baking at Heligan has certainly evolved over recent years, from the early days at Heligan, when to make a few scones and cakes was all that was required and to sell 100 portions was a big event, to the present day, with our purpose-built bakery producing home made bread, scones, various morning goods and up to a staggering 14,000 slices of cake a week.

Quality is very important to us. Whether it's one of the thousands of cakes eaten by our day visitors, a tempting dessert served on 'Feast Night' or one of the hundreds of festive goodies sold to take away, great pride and care is given to every item we produce. It is our passion for good food, quality ingredients and home-grown produce that has given the catering at Heligan its hallmark.

This book is packed full of irresistible cakes, fragrant breads, indulgent desserts, afternoon teatime treats and much more. All are tried, tested and used on a regular basis here at Heligan. In the bakery we are not quite as driven by the seasons as in the main kitchen, where menus are planned around what's available from the productive gardens. Here many recipes stand on their own merit without the use of home-grown ingredients; but make no mistake, whenever fresh fruit arrives from the garden there is great excitement and the resulting buns or cakes sell out fast. Our breads are also transformed by the copious amounts of fresh herbs readily available. The aroma from the baking sets people's heads swimming and tummies a-rumbling.

Baking with home-grown produce gives us a vital link with the gardens. Visitors can not only explore the productive acres, but also experience the taste of Heligan. The skilful team of gardeners must not be forgotten. Without their year-round dedication and depth of horticultural knowledge we would not be cooking in what we call 'chef's heaven'.

We have arranged the sections of this book in the order in which we cook the items daily; starting early in the morning, through to the busy afternoon, and then on into the evening. Each one loosely arranged in seasonal order, these sections are as follows:

Morning Bakery

Arriving in the small hours is such a pleasure: the dew on the grass, the early morning mist rising and the air full of birdsong; this is when Heligan is at its best. Soon the smell of freshly baked bread fills the morning air. Add to this the scones, Heligan buns and bread rolls packed with home grown herbs, by 9 o'clock the aroma from the bakery fills our little bit of Cornwall. These recipes which start our day include saffron buns, sweet and savoury scones, and some fine continental style breads.

Afternoon Delights

With the birdsong long forgotten, afternoon tea can be a very busy time. Hundreds of cakes go in a flash, huge baskets of scones disappear in minutes; keeping up with this is hard work but very rewarding. When our customers ask for recipes on a daily basis and local people come for afternoon tea with no intention of going in the gardens, we must be doing something right. Tempting tea-time treats, like pungent ginger cake, very moreish brownies, rich dark Heligan fruit cake and a carrot cake to die for, are recipes you will want to use again and again.

Just Desserts

On Friday Feast Nights the Willows Tearoom turns into a vine clad restaurant, with candlelit tables, some good jazz, fine wine and cooking with the best of Cornish produce, regularly including our own farmed meat, vegetables, fruit and herbs. For these evenings we go one step further and produce some mouth watering desserts, like the classic summer pudding, feather light citrus house soufflé, and the deliciously different, rose petal and peach cheesecake. Made with home grown ingredients and impeccably presented, these are puds to impress!

Festive Fare

At certain times of the year our daily routine receives a welcome interruption. Festive celebrations have always included 'feasting' in some way; hot cross buns and Christmas cake are the most common examples. Here we also include handmade chocolates, marzipan fruits, coconut ice, Simnel cake and figgy pudding, to name but a few. Whatever the occasion : 'bake a cake' — that's our motto!

On the pages that follow we hope not only to share our closely guarded recipes with you, but also to give a glimpse of life here at Heligan and introduce some of its characters. We wish you every culinary success; have fun and happy baking.

The Recipes

Morning Bakery

Afternoon Delights

Just Desserts

Festive Fare

Italian Style Ramson Bread

Ramsons (or wild garlic) grow just about everywhere down here in Cornwall. Woodland walks are suddenly bathed in the heady aroma of garlic. You don't need to look for ramsons, just follow your nose and they will find you! Ramsons to my mind are literally manna from heaven. This bread recipe uses olive oil and produces a Mediterranean-style bread infused with wild garlic. (PD)

For 2 loaves

900g/2lb strong plain flour
55g/2oz fresh yeast
4 tablespoons olive oil
1 teaspoon salt
455mls/16fl oz warm water
170g/6oz shredded ramson leaves
55g/2oz chopped green pitted olives
2 teaspoons caster sugar

Dissolve the yeast and sugar in the warm water, sift the flour and salt into a mixing bowl making a well in the centre. Pour in the yeast mixture, olive oil, shredded ramsons and chopped green olives.

Flick some flour from the edge of the bowl to cover the surface of the liquid. Cover with a cloth and move to a warm place for 10 minutes until bubbles form on the surface. Stir the mixture to form a rough dough, turn out onto a floured table and knead the dough until smooth and free from any stickiness. Return to the bowl, cover with a cloth and leave to prove in a warm place for 20 minutes or until doubled in size. Turn onto the floured table and knead for a second time for at least 5 minutes until smooth and even in texture. Shape into two long, flattish loaves, rather like a ciabatta in shape. Place on a greased baking tray, cutting the top with a sharp knife making diagonal incisions about half an inch deep. Brush with a little olive oil and leave to rise in a warm place until almost double in size. Bake in a preheated oven 220°C/425°F/gas 7 for 10 minutes, then turn down to 180°C/350°F/gas 4 for 15–20 minutes until golden brown and sounds hollow when tapped underneath. Move onto a wire cooling rack and leave for at least half an hour before cutting. This bread is excellent with pasta and perfect for making bruschetta. Just cut into slices and toast in the oven until crisp, rub with a clove of garlic, drizzle with a little olive oil, garnish with some fresh basil and it's ready.

Basic Bread Dough – Baked in Flowerpots!

One of the most important things that any baker has to learn is the recipe for a basic bread dough. Over the years I have tried many, but this one stands out as one of the best. It serves its purpose well for loaves or rolls but the addition of herbs, cheeses, or even the trendy sun-dried tomato, equip you with a whole range of breads to send your taste buds racing. We have used the flowerpot idea in a couple of recipes (see the Potty Heligan Fruit Cake) and it just gives the plainest recipe a novel and fun edge. (TB)

For 4 loaves

900g/2lb strong white flour
55g/2oz fresh yeast
55g/2oz butter
570mls/1pt warm water
2 teaspoons caster sugar
1 teaspoon salt
1 egg
poppy seeds for decoration
4 x 11.5cms/4½ins clay pots

Sift the flour and salt into a large bowl, rub in the butter, then make a well in the centre of the mix. Dissolve the sugar and yeast into the water and add the egg to this. Add a bit at a time to your flour mix and bring together until a soft dough has formed. Cover this with a damp cloth and leave to rise until it has doubled in size. Turn out onto a lightly floured table and knead for 5–10 minutes – this is called 'knocking back' – or until smooth. Divide into balls big enough to half fill your clay pots. Place dough in the pots and leave to prove until the dough has risen just above the rim of the pot. Glaze with some beaten egg and sprinkle on some poppy seeds. Bake in a pre-heated oven at 180°C/350°F/gas 4 until golden brown. Once the bread is turned out of the pots it should sound hollow when tapped underneath.

It is essential to season your pots
Take some clay pots of your preferred size and brush with vegetable or sunflower oil. Bake in a pre-heated oven at 200°C/400°F/gas 6 for 15 minutes, then leave to cool. Repeat this process six times. (This seems a lot, but once your pots are seasoned you can use them over and over again).

Tri-colour Bread Plait

This recipe sounds quite complicated but is well worth the effort; it is ideal for a dinner party and can be made in miniature to form little plaited rolls. Tina made these for some of the Feast Nights at Heligan, but looking back, not all her cooking has been this elaborate. Soon after starting at Heligan she turned up for work early one morning only to find a note from myself informing her that Tim Smit and some VIPs were keen to experience a traditional Cornish breakfast. I included a genuine recipe for 'Gurty Grey' which she diligently followed, only to find our 'guests' did not show. We did not expect Tina to make what, after all, is simply a saucepan of cooked flour and water... It was only a prank on my part but a sore point with her to this day! (PD)

For 2 loaves

1 x basic bread dough mixture (see page 7)
2 tablespoons tomato purée
2 tablespoons green pesto
a little plain flour

After making the basic bread dough, divide into 3 equal parts, putting one aside. Mix the tomato purée into the second piece and the green pesto into the third piece, kneading with a little flour to bring back to the correct consistency. Divide each piece into two, rolling each into a long thin sausage shape. Line up the red, white and green pieces of dough and plait into a loaf about 38cms/15ins long. Repeat with the other 3 lengths – place the loaves on a lightly greased baking tray and allow to prove in a warm place until doubled in size. Bake in a preheated oven 200°C/400°F/gas 6 for 10 minutes then turn down to 170°C/325°F/gas 3 for a further 10–15 minutes until golden and sounding hollow when tapped underneath. Allow to cool before cutting.

Sun-dried Tomato and Rosemary Bread

Rosemary is such a wonderful herb, with a powerful, intensely aromatic character. Superb with roast lamb and pork, excellent in stuffings and risottos, you can even use it in sweet dishes. This herb has endless possibilities. In 1826 Dr. Culpeper claimed rosemary to be a miracle cure from head to toe. However, I am not sure about his claim that a 'decoction of rosemary and wine will cure stupidness...' So here's my very fragrant and flavoursome bread recipe and, who knows, that 'stupidness' could be a thing of the past! (PD)

For 2 loaves

900g/2lb strong white bread flour
110g/4oz sun-dried tomatoes (in olive oil)
55g/2oz fresh yeast
2 teaspoons caster sugar
1 teaspoon salt
1 egg
570mls/1pt warm water
10 large sprigs fresh rosemary

Try making some rosemary sugar by inserting fresh sprigs of rosemary into a jar of caster sugar and leaving it for at least a month. Use this in syrups, custards and sorbets, or best of all make poached pears with rosemary and sherry

Sift the flour and salt into a large mixing bowl, making a well in the centre. Dissolve the yeast and sugar into the warm water and pour this along with the egg into the well in your flour. Place the rosemary into the liquid (having removed the woody stalks) along with 2 fluid ounces of the olive oil from the jar of sun dried tomatoes (this contains lots of flavour). Remove the tomatoes from the oil and chop roughly – add these to the liquid and flick flour from around the edges to cover the surface. Cover with a damp cloth and leave in a warm place until bubbles have broken the surface. Mix into a rough dough, cover and return to a warm place to prove until doubled in size. Turn this onto a lightly floured table and knead for 4–5 minutes until smooth and free from stickiness. Divide into 2 and shape into balls. Carefully place these on a lightly greased baking tray, cut a shallow cross in the top, dust with a little flour and leave to prove in a warm place until doubled in size. Bake in a preheated oven 220°C/425°F/gas 7 for 10 minutes, then turn down to 180°C/350°F/gas 4 for a further 20 minutes until golden and sounding hollow when tapped underneath. Cool on a wire rack before cutting.

Roast Vegetable Calzone

Being a chef with Italian roots I find myself drawn to the warmth of Mediterranean flavours. When pungent fresh herbs are paired with olive oil, roast peppers, tomatoes and a good red wine, a quick lunchtime snack can turn into a long relaxed meal running well into the afternoon. Some of our breads in particular have an Italian feel. The aromas and flavours from our home-grown herbs lend themselves beautifully to this style of bread. If only we could grow olives here...Calzone is not so much a bread but a folded pizza, and a pizza in the true sense is nothing like you find on the supermarket shelves. (PD)

For 2 loaves

900g/2lb strong white bread flour
55g/2oz fresh yeast
1 teaspoon salt
500mls/18fl oz warm water
2 teaspoons sugar
4 tablespoons fruity virgin olive oil
1 egg
1 small courgette
1 red pepper
1 red onion
2 tomatoes
1 large bunch fresh basil
1 small bunch oregano
1 small bunch parsley
cracked sea salt

Dice the courgette, red pepper and onion, place in a small roasting tray and drizzle with a little olive oil. Roast in a preheated oven 200°C/400°F/gas 6 for 10–15 minutes until just browning on the edges. Remove and allow to cool. Sift the flour and the salt into a large mixing bowl. Make a well in the centre, dissolve the yeast and sugar in warm water and pour this, along with 2 tablespoons of olive oil and the egg, into the well. Finely chop the fresh herbs and stir into the liquid. Flick some flour from around the edge of the bowl to cover the surface. Move to a warm place, covering with a damp cloth and leave until bubbles are breaking the surface. When this happens, work the mixture into a rough dough before covering and returning to a warm place to prove. When the dough has doubled in size turn it onto a lightly floured table. Knead well for 4–5 minutes until smooth and free from stickiness. Divide in half, shaping each into a ball; then, using the knuckles of one hand, spread out into two flat ovals before spreading the vegetables over half of each one. Slice the tomatoes and spread these over the top of the roast vegetables. Fold over, sealing each along the edge. Place onto a lightly greased baking tray and, using the fingertips, push deep indentations over the surface, drizzle with the remaining olive oil and sprinkle with a little cracked sea salt. Allow to prove in a warm place until almost double in size, then bake in a preheated oven 200°C/400°F/gas 6 for 20–30 minutes until golden brown and sounding hollow when tapped underneath. This bread goes perfectly with pasta and red pesto (see A *Taste of Heligan : vegetarian and fruit recipes*).

Summer Savory and Sunflower Bread

Until I came to Heligan I had not used this herb a great deal. I mainly associated savory with bean dishes, like cassoulet; in fact the German word for savory is bohnenkraut (meaning bean-herb). I soon found summer savory went very well with meats of every description, but this bread lets you enjoy the intense flavour of the herb in its own right. Served with soups, casseroles or pasta, it is a bread well worth making. The taste just conjures up busy summer Feast Nights at Heligan – I can almost hear the jazz! (PD)

For 2 loaves

900g/2lb strong plain flour
1 teaspoon salt
55g/2oz fresh yeast
2 teaspoons caster sugar
570g/1pt warm water
30g/1oz melted butter
55g/2oz chopped summer savory
85g/3oz sunflower seeds

Sift the flour and salt into a mixing bowl and make a well in the centre. Mix the yeast into the warm water with the sugar and melted butter. Pour this into the well, add the sunflower seeds and finely chopped summer savory. Flick flour from the edge of the bowl to cover the liquid. Move to a warm place, cover with a cloth and leave for approximately 10 minutes, until bubbles start to form on the surface. Mix into a rough dough and turn onto a floured table. Knead for about 5 minutes until all the stickiness has gone. Return to the bowl, cover and leave for 20 minutes in a warm place until doubled in size. Turn onto the floured table and knead a second time, shape into 2 large balls and 2 small balls. Place the larger onto a lightly greased baking sheet then on top of each place a smaller ball of dough. Dip your finger into flour and push down through the very centre of each loaf until you touch the baking tray. This should present you with 2 cottage-style loaves. Leave in a warm place until almost doubled in size. Then bake in a preheated oven – 200°C/400°F/gas 6 for 15 minutes and turn down to 180°C/350°F/gas 4 for a further 15–20 minutes until golden brown and hollow-sounding when tapped underneath. Leave to cool on a wire rack for at least half an hour before cutting. We serve this bread with homemade hummus bi tahini, a Greek dip made with chick peas, tahini, olive oil, garlic and coriander.

Black Olive and Lemon Thyme Focaccia

Olives! You either love them or you hate them, and just for the record, I think they are food from the gods. But in the other camp there is much turning up of noses and prize-winning gurning when olives are mentioned. But how many of these people have tasted real good quality olives? If your olives are in brine, you should decant them, drain carefully and throw them away! The majority of olives eaten by us Brits over the years have been in brine and brine is all you can taste. Olives must be in olive oil – buy yourself some nice sweet little black olives, maybe marinated with lemon and herbs, eat one of these and I hope you will be converted. (PD)

For 2 loaves

900g/2lb strong unbleached bread flour
515mls/18fl oz warm water
1 teaspoon salt
55g/2oz fresh yeast
2 teaspoons sugar
110g/4oz pitted black olives
6 tablespoons fruity olive oil
1 egg
1 large bunch fresh lemon thyme
zest of 1 lemon
cracked sea salt

Sift the flour and salt into a large mixing bowl and make a well in the centre. Dissolve the yeast and sugar in the warm water before stirring in the egg, 3 tablespoons of olive oil, lemon zest, black olives and the lemon thyme removed from its stalks. Pour this mixture into the well in the flour and flick a little flour from around the edges to cover the surface. Place a damp cloth over the top, move to a warm place, leaving until bubbles are breaking the surface. When this happens mix into a rough dough, cover and return to a warm place until risen and doubled in size. Turn dough onto a floured table and knead for 5 minutes until smooth and free from stickiness. Cut dough in half and shape into 2 large flat circles about 2cms/1in thick. Place on a lightly greased baking tray and, using the fingers, push indentations over each loaf. Then drizzle with the remaining olive oil and sprinkle with cracked sea salt. Prove in a warm place until almost doubled in size, cook in a preheated oven 220°C/425°F/gas 7 for 10 minutes and then turn down to 180°C/350°/gas 4 for 15 minutes or until golden and hollow sounding when tapped underneath. Allow to cool on a wire rack. This bread is wonderful served with a fruity red wine, ripe brie and vine tomatoes.

Heligan Honey Ale Bread

This is a wonderfully malty, nutty bread and the smell is just so intoxicating. This goes well with any home-made soup but especially the hearty winter broth style soups – this is 'comfort food' at its best. Our very own honey ale was used to replace the water in this recipe, but feel free to substitute this with your favourite local brew! (PD)

For 2 loaves

900g/2lb malted granary flour
55g/2oz melted butter
570mls/1pt warm honey ale
55g/2oz fresh yeast
2 teaspoons malt extract
2 teaspoons demerara sugar
generous pinch of salt
a little plain flour

Dissolve the yeast, malt extract and sugar in the warm beer, put the flour in a mixing bowl with a pinch of salt and make a well in the centre. Pour in the beer and yeast mixture and add the melted butter. Flick some of the flour from the edge of the bowl to cover the surface of the liquid. Cover with a tea towel and leave somewhere warm for 10 minutes until bubbles start to rise to the surface. Mix well and knead into a smooth dough that's free from stickiness. You may need to add a little plain flour depending on the strength of flour you are using. When the consistency is right, cover again and put somewhere warm to prove. This may take 20–30 minutes or until the dough doubles in size. Then turn out onto a floured table and knead again. Mould the dough into two perfect balls and put on a lightly greased baking sheet. Cut a cross in the top and lightly dust with plain flour. Leave in a warm place to rise. When the dough has doubled in size bake in a hot oven 200°C/400°F/gas 6 for 15 minutes, then turn down to 180°C/350°F/gas 4 for 10 minutes. If you tap the bottom of the loaf and it sounds hollow then it should be done. Put on a wire rack to cool before slicing.

Please do not spread margarine on this bread! If one goes to the trouble of baking one's own bread then only real butter will do it justice.

Heligan Buns

I invented these delicious buns in my first summer at Heligan. I took the traditional saffron bun and jazzed it up a little with the addition of fresh root ginger and a zing of rough-cut marmalade. As soon as the Heligan buns go on display at the Willows Tea Rooms it is just a matter of minutes until they are all sold out. We just can't make them fast enough! (PD)

For 12 buns

450g/1lb plain flour
a large pinch saffron
30g/1oz fresh yeast
110g/4oz caster sugar
110g/4oz melted butter
240mls/8fl oz milk
1 egg
55g/2oz currants
2cms/1in piece root ginger
110g/4oz rough-cut marmalade
Pinch of salt

Heat the milk, stirring in the saffron, simmer for 1 minute and allow to cool until just warm. Sift the flour and salt into a mixing bowl and make a well in the centre. Mix the yeast in with the milk adding the beaten egg, half the melted butter and half the sugar and then pour into the well in the flour. Beat thoroughly until smooth and elastic. Cover with a cloth and put in a warm place to rise until doubled in size for about 40 minutes.

Turn the dough onto a floured table and roll out into an oblong shape. Brush with the remaining butter, fold and roll out again into a 46cms/18ins square. Peel and grate the ginger and mix it into the marmalade, then spread over the bun dough. Sprinkle the currants evenly over the marmalade then roll up like a Swiss roll. Cut into 1½in slices and place flat side up close together on a greased baking tray. Move to a warm place to prove for 20 minutes or until almost doubled in size. Sprinkle with the remaining sugar and bake in a preheated oven at 200°C/400°F/gas 6 for 20–25 minutes when they should be golden brown.

Cool on a wire rack for at least half an hour – if you can resist them that long! Serve with a pot of your favourite tea.

Saffron Buns

Saffron is the world's most expensive spice. Many years ago, merchants traded saffron for tin, and this was its probable introduction into the Cornish culinary line-up. It can also be used as a sedative and is even fatal in large doses. Many a Cornish mother has signed the National Poisons Register in order to gain permission for her children to eat saffron cake! (TB)

For 12 buns

675g/1½lb strong white flour
30g/1oz fresh yeast
55g/2oz caster sugar
85g/3oz butter
55g/2oz sultanas
55g/2oz currants
290mls/10fl oz milk
½ teaspoon salt
1 small sachet saffron (as sold in any delicatessen)

Heat half of the milk in a saucepan until near boiling. Remove from the heat and add the saffron, leaving to soak for around 30 minutes. In a large mixing bowl rub the butter into the flour and salt. Warm the remaining milk and add the yeast and caster sugar. Slowly mix the saffron milk and the yeast milk into the flour mixture until you have a soft dough. Cover with a damp cloth and leave to rise until doubled in size. Turn the dough onto a lightly floured table and knead in the sultanas and currants. Divide the dough, roll into balls and place on a greased and floured baking tray, leaving to prove until doubled in size. Bake in a pre-heated oven at 190°C/375°F/gas 5 for 10–15 minutes or until golden. Leave to cool on a wire rack.

Plain Scones

Any good baker's stalwart recipe, this one is quick, straightforward and can be used as a base for many other flavoured scones. However, my advice to you is that you bake these plain, get some homemade strawberry jam and lashings of real Cornish clotted cream...and brew a pot of tea. An absolute must for those lazy, hot summer teatimes. (TB)

For 6–8 large scones

450g/1lb self-raising flour
110g/4oz caster sugar
225g/8oz butter
150mls/5fl oz milk
3 teaspoons baking powder

Put the flour, sugar and baking powder into a bowl, rub in the butter and then gradually add the milk, little by little, until a soft dough is formed. Knead lightly then roll out, on a floured table, to about 1cm/^{1}/$_2$in thickness. Cut out the scones using a cookie cutter, and place on a tray lined with baking paper. Brush the tops of the scones with milk then bake in a pre-heated oven at 180°C/350°F/gas 4 for 15–20 minutes. Leave to cool on a wire rack.

At certain times during the season, we have an abundance of berries from our gardens here at Heligan. Try adding these to the mix or maybe some fresh rhubarb, which has been lightly pre-cooked.

Cheese Scones

To put a savoury slant on the scone recipe try adding some herbs, such as chives, or sun-dried tomatoes. When we experimented with the tomato recipe, I let my dad try some. He had been in catering for years and said that they would never work – we sold thousands! (TB)

For 6–8 large scones

450g/1lb self-raising flour
225g/8oz butter
340g/12oz grated cheese (of your choice)
150mls/5fl oz milk
3 teaspoons baking powder

Place the flour, baking powder and 8oz of the cheese into a bowl, mix together then rub in the butter. Add your milk, little by little, until a soft dough is formed. Knead lightly then roll out, on a floured table, to about 1cm/½in thickness. Cut out the scones using a cookie cutter, and place on a tray lined with baking paper. Brush the tops of the scones with milk and sprinkle on the remaining 4oz of cheese. Bake in a pre-heated oven at 180°C/350°F/gas 4 for 15–20 minutes. Leave to cool on a wire rack.

As an alternative, try using some goats' cheese and adding pine kernels.

17

Apple and Quince Turnovers

You can use any fruit in this recipe – rhubarb or summer fruits for example – but we use apples and quinces from our gardens. Did you know that the quince is dedicated to Venus and is a symbol of love and happiness? Personally, I serve these with lashings of Cornish clotted cream and that provides me with all the happiness that I need for that moment. You may notice, shock horror, that I am using bought puff pastry for this recipe! To be honest, it's just as good as anything you could spend hours making, so don't feel that you're cheating – just occasionally, convenience is also best! (TB)

For 6–8 turnovers

225g/8oz bought puff pastry
450g/1lb cooking apples
55g/2oz caster sugar
1 quince
1 egg
a little icing sugar

Peel, core and chop the apples and quince and place in a large pan with a splash of water and the caster sugar. Cover and cook gently until the apple is soft, then leave to cool. On a floured table, roll out the puff pastry to about 3mm/⅛in thickness and cut into 10cms/4ins circles with a cookie cutter. Place a couple of good tablespoons of the fruit into the middle of the pastry circle and then fold over, very much like a pasty, sealing the edges with a little egg wash. Take care to make sure that the parcel is properly sealed. Repeat this until you run out of pastry or fruit. Egg wash the tops of the parcels and place on a baking tray that has been lined with baking paper. Bake in a pre-heated oven at 180°C/350°F/gas 4 for 20–25 minutes until golden brown. Once cooled, dust with icing sugar.

Clotted Cream Shortbread

Due to the huge demand for our fresh baked goods, an extended bakery has been installed at Heligan. Kieron, one of our existing staff, has signed up as trainee baker. Being very interested in his new profession, he takes it upon himself to sample everything in order to familiarise himself with how they should taste when he is let loose. This shortbread recipe is the one he is most 'familiar' with. Kieron is so enthisiastic in his tasting that we have decided to weigh him at the end of the season. We all have a little book running on the end result. Strangely enough no one has gone for a loss! (TB)

For 10–12 portions

225g/8oz butter
225g/8oz clotted cream
340g/12oz caster sugar
450g/1lb plain flour

Place the butter, clotted cream and sugar into a food mixer and beat until light. Add the flour and mix for 1 minute. Grease and lightly flour a 25.5cms/10ins flan tin and press the mixture into it, ensuring an even thickness. Mark the top of the mixture with a fork to a pattern of your choice, then place into a pre-heated oven at 150°C/300°F/gas 2 for 35–40 minutes. The shortbread should be lightly golden in colour. Cut into portions whilst it is still hot, sprinkle with caster sugar and leave to cool.

We sometimes add dried strawberries to the mix, which is always popular, but for that totally indulgent touch use a couple of shortbread rounds to make a sandwich filled to bursting with whipped cream and fresh fruit.

Gingerbread Women!

Gingerbread biscuits have always been baked in all shapes and sizes. All of us I'm sure remember the childhood tales of The Gingerbread Man *and* Hansel and Gretel *with their gingerbread house. Why gingerbread has such a prominent place in folklore and fairy tales isn't really evident but we do know that ginger was a spice used to combat the effects of the plague. (TB)*

For 12–15 dependent on cutter size

285g/10oz plain flour
170g/6oz dark brown sugar
110g/4oz golden syrup
40mls/1½fl oz water
4 teaspoons ground ginger
2 teaspoons mixed spice
1 teaspoon baking powder
1 teaspoon bicarbonate of soda
currants (for the eyes)

Bring together all of the dry ingredients in a food mixer. Add the butter, syrup and water and mix until a soft dough is formed. Wrap in cling film and leave to chill in a fridge for around 2 hours. Roll out on a lightly floured table until 5mm/¼in thick and press shapes out with your cutter. Place them on a tray lined with baking paper, add the eyes (currants) and bake in a pre-heated oven at 180°C/350°F/gas 4 for 10–15 minutes. Leave to cool.

Muesli Bars

Unfortunately some of us cannot enjoy cake to its full potential because of dietary restriction. However this gluten free recipe offers a sound alternative to the honey flapjack. Because we bake in such huge quantities, most of our recipes are as simple as possible and this one is no exception. (TB)

For 8–10 bars

450g/1lb rolled oats
340g/12oz honey
170g/6oz margarine
55g/2oz caster sugar
55g/2oz sunflower seeds
55g/2oz chopped dried dates
55g/2oz chopped dried apricots
55g/2oz chopped glacé cherries
55g/2oz chopped mixed nuts

Melt the margarine and honey together. In a separate bowl, mix together the remaining ingredients. Combine the two mixes and place into a lined, shallow tin 30cms/12ins x 37.5cms/15ins, making sure you press down firmly to an even spread. Bake in a pre-heated oven at 180°C/350°F/gas 4 for 15–20 minutes until lightly browned. Cut into portions whilst hot, then leave to cool.

This is gluten free

Honey and Sunflower Seed Flapjack

Tasty, quick and it does the trick! Keep this recipe handy for those emergency times. For a bit of variety try replacing the sunflower seeds with cranberries or flaked almonds. In the height of our summer season, I make at least 24 large trays a day of this recipe alone. That's a staggering 768 flapjacks! (TB)

For 8–10 portions

450g/1lb rolled oats
55g/2oz caster sugar
170g/6oz sunflower seeds
170g/6oz margarine
340g/12oz honey

Mix together the rolled oats, caster sugar and sunflower seeds. Melt the margarine and honey together then add to the other ingredients and mix thoroughly. Lightly press into a lined, shallow baking tray 30cms/12ins x 37.5cms/15ins and place in a pre-heated oven at 180°C /350°F/gas 4 for 10–15 minutes until lightly coloured. Cut into portions whilst hot and allow to cool.

This is gluten free

Caramel Slices

This was one of the very first recipes I made at Heligan and now it is the first one I teach any trainee, as it tends to drive me potty, standing for hours, making the caramel. However, this recipe does come with a special tip for the ladies. According to our very own Sue Bishop, if you want something sweet to lead the way to a man's heart, this is it! (TB)

For 8–10 slices

For the base
225g/8oz margarine
170g/6oz plain flour
170g/6oz rolled oats
110g/4oz caster sugar

For the caramel and topping
450g/1lb chocolate
170g/6oz margarine
110g/4oz dark brown sugar
1 x 397g tin of condensed milk

To make the base, place the margarine and caster sugar into a food mixer and beat until pale and light. Add the flour and rolled oats and mix for a further minute. Press the mix into a shallow, lined baking tray 30cms/12ins x 37.5cms/15ins and bake in a pre-heated oven at 180°C/350°F/gas 4 for 15–20 minutes or until lightly browned. Leave to cool.

Then make the caramel: put the margarine, dark brown sugar and condensed milk into a metal saucepan. Bring to the boil, stirring continuously, and boil for five minutes until a thick texture has formed.

Assemble by spreading the caramel over the base evenly and right up to the edges. Leave to cool. Melt the chocolate and pour over the top of the caramel, again spreading completely. Once the chocolate has set, cut into portions of your preferred size.

Date and Oat Slice

This is the most versatile of recipes, producing one of our esteemed customer's favourite cakes. The dates can be replaced with stewed apricots for a bit of extra 'zing'! I think that rhubarb would also make a tasty alternative when in season. We made some with figs last Christmas which went down a treat. (TB)

For 8–10 slices

450g/1lb plain flour
225g/8oz rolled oats
225g/8oz dark brown sugar
110g/4oz caster sugar
340g/12oz margarine
900g/2lb dried dates

Place the flour, oats, caster and dark brown sugar into a bowl and mix well. Melt the margarine, add to the dry mixture then divide this into two. Meanwhile, place the dates into a saucepan, just covering them with water, and simmer until soft. Cover the base of a lined, shallow tin 30cms/12ins x 37.5cms/15ins with one half of the mixture and press down. Take the stewed dates and spread them evenly over the top. The remaining mixture can now be used to cover the dates. Bake in a pre-heated oven at 180°C/350°F/gas 4 for 30–40 minutes. Cut when cooled.

Coconut Pyramids and Almond Macaroons

I paired these recipes together as they are quite similar: wheat-free and both with a heavy, nutty flavour popular with our visitors. These days dietary requirements are becoming more important all the time. We can happily accommodate vegans, coeliacs, diabetics etc. However, a customer recently asked if we had any cakes without flour, sugar, eggs, and dairy-free... I must admit I was completely at a loss as to what to recommend and could only offer the fruit basket. So if anybody has such a recipe, I would be very pleased to hear from them, just in case that gentleman returns. (PD)

For 8–10

For the pyramids
225g/8oz desiccated coconut
225g/8oz caster sugar
2 eggs
5 glacé cherries

For the macaroons
110g/4oz ground almonds
170g/6oz caster sugar
30g/1oz ground rice
2 egg whites
10 whole blanched almonds

To make the pyramids, first mix the coconut, sugar and eggs thoroughly in a food mixer. Wet a dariole mould, fill tightly with the mixture and with a sharp tap, turn out onto a lightly greased baking sheet. Continue this with all the mix and decorate each pyramid with half a glacé cherry. Bake in a preheated oven 170°C/325°F/gas 3 for 15–20 minutes, but keep an eye on them as they burn easily. When golden-brown remove from the oven and allow to cool completely before moving them, and store in an airtight tin.

Then on to the macaroons. Place the ground almonds, sugar, egg-whites and ground rice into a food mixer, beat for a few minutes until thoroughly mixed. Grease and line a baking sheet and spoon the mixture into little piles, spaced well apart (when baking they will spread out). Place a whole almond in the centre of each mound and bake in a preheated oven 180°C/350°F/gas 4 for 18–20 minutes until golden-brown, remove from the oven and allow to cool completely before moving. Store in an airtight tin.

Ginger Cake

A truly old-fashioned cake in which everything is simply mixed together and baked, leaving a wonderful aroma floating around for hours. It has to be said that the flavour of this cake improves greatly if kept over several days, although if you're anything like me, it won't last ten minutes. Apparently this cake is excellent for settling your stomach, good if you have morning sickness for example, although that is a pretty radical excuse for just eating cake! (TB)

For 6–8 portions

110g/4oz margarine
110g/10oz dark brown sugar
200g/7oz golden syrup
225g/8oz plain flour
150mls/5fl oz milk
5 teaspoons ground ginger
1 teaspoon bicarbonate of soda
1 egg

Place all of the ingredients into a food mixer and beat together until thoroughly mixed. Put this into a medium depth, lined baking tray 30cms/12ins x 37.5cms/15ins and bake in a pre-heated oven at 150°C/300°F/gas 2 for 40–50 minutes until light and springy to the touch. Leave to cool then cut into portions.

Carrot Cake

A carrot cake made well can be as good as any high class dessert in a Michelin starred restaurant. I say 'made well' because quite often I come across very poor examples! A good indication of any tearoom is the quality of its carrot cake. I once had a superb wedge of carrot cake down at Lamorna Cove one morning, only to find myself at a nearby garden attraction that afternoon, presented with a monstrosity obviously made from a packet mix, and topped with a full inch of butter cream, but made with cheap margarine. There really is no excuse for this when you see how delightfully simple this recipe is. (PD)

For 12–15 portions

For the carrot cake
225g/8oz grated carrot
340g/12oz self-raising flour
285g/10oz caster sugar
55g/2oz chopped nuts
a few drops of vanilla essence
6 eggs
3 teaspoons ground cinnamon
2 teaspoons ground ginger
350mls/12fl oz sunflower oil
1 teaspoon baking powder

For the frosting
170g/6oz cream cheese
225g/8oz icing sugar
1 tablespoon lemon juice

Take all the cake ingredients, put them in a large mixing bowl and give them a really good stir. You can't get much easier than that, can you! Spread out the mixture in a greased, lined baking tin (large and quite shallow – 30cms/12ins x 37.5cms/15ins, bake in a preheated oven 170°C/325°F/gas 3 for 30–35 minutes – test with a sharp knife and if it comes out clean it's done; if not, cook a little longer. When cooked, remove from the oven and allow to cool completely before applying the frosting. This again is a case of placing all the frosting ingredients in a mixing bowl, beating thoroughly with a spoon or hand held food mixer until light, smooth and even-textured. Spoon onto the cake and spread out with a palette knife before cutting into portions.

At Heligan we garnish each piece with a tiny marzipan carrot.

This recipe could not be easier, but why stop at carrot cake? Try replacing the same weight of carrots with grated apple, mashed banana or, most surprisingly of all – parsnip! Some people have turned their noses up at my parsnip cake, but when forced to try a slice, they always come back for a large helping of humble pie, so don't be afraid to try it!

Chocolate Nut Brownie

Always use a good chocolate in this recipe because you really can taste the difference, and you also feel just that little bit more indulgent when you finally tuck in! It is also a well-documented fact that nuns and monks who fasted throughout Lent ate only chocolate, due to its nutritional value. Any excuse! (TB)

For 12–15 portions

450g/1lb butter
450g/1lb melted chocolate
675g/1½lb caster sugar
225g/8oz self-raising flour
85g/3oz chopped nuts (omit if you'd rather)
10 eggs

For decoration
2 tablespoons cocoa powder

Place the butter and caster sugar into a bowl and cream together with a beater until light and fluffy. Add the melted chocolate, flour, nuts and eggs and mix well. Line a shallow tin – 30cms/12ins x 37.5cms/15ins with greaseproof paper and spread in the mixture. Bake in a pre-heated oven at 180°C/350°F/gas 4 for 40–50 minutes. Cut once cooled and dust with cocoa powder.

Beer and Banana Bread Pudding

Bread pudding always goes well at the Willows Tearoom, but being a chef I can't help experimenting, so far resulting in varieties such as apple, cinnamon and scrumpy, date and orange, and even tomato, cheddar and basil. Here the marriage of Cornish real ale, ripe bananas and warm spices is a match made in heaven. (PD)

For 8–10 portions

1 small granary bloomer (3 days old is best!)
570mls/1 pint real ale (we use Betty Stoggs)
2 eggs
85g/3oz sultanas
110g/4oz demerara sugar
30g/10oz caster sugar
85g/3oz butter
4 ripe bananas
3 teaspoons ground cinnamon
half a teaspoon ground nutmeg
half a teaspoon ginger

Grease and line a large baking tray with raised sides. Break the bread into a large mixing bowl, then, while mixing with one hand, gradually pour the beer in with the other. Only add as much beer as it takes to thoroughly moisten the bread. Don't make it too wet – you may need less than a pint, but I'm sure you will find a use for the rest! Peel and break up the bananas; add these along with the egg, demerara sugar, butter, spices and sultanas to the bread. Mix thoroughly and turn onto the baking tray. Spread out evenly and bake in a preheated oven 180°C/350°F/gas 4 for 45 minutes to 1 hour, or until browned and slightly firm to touch. Serve hot or cold, sprinkled with caster sugar, but be warned, the smell from this is quite intoxicating!

While numerous varieties of herbs are grown at Heligan, spices are something more suited to a much hotter climate. So when Richard (the previous catering manager) began parading around the kitchen proudly holding aloft the first ever Heligan grown Giant Nutmeg it caused much excitement. I was particularly pleased, as I had placed the avocado stone along with a fake gardeners' note in his in-tray only an hour before!

Cranberry Muffins

Muffins are easily the most popular cake that I make here at Heligan and during the summer season we sell literally thousands of them. It does have to be noted, however, that I make even more than we sell as Richard, our previous catering manager, had a soft spot for them and could easily eat six or seven in a day! Of course, he never admitted it. Although I have used cranberries for this recipe, you can add just about anything you have in your store cupboard at home – chocolate drops, fruit and spice or dried apricots. We have used berries from the garden. However, for something a little different, and if you're feeling exotic, why not try dried pineapple or coconut. (TB)

For 8–10 muffins

340g/12oz self-raising flour
170g/6oz caster sugar
110g/4oz butter
110g/4oz dried cranberries
190mls/6½fl oz milk
2 eggs

Melt the butter – in a microwave is easier, if you have one – then add all of the ingredients together in a food mixer. Mix for 1–2 minutes. Fill your muffin cases to the top and bake in a pre-heated oven at 180°C/350°F/gas 4 for 10–15 minutes, until they spring back when pressed. Leave to cool on a wire rack then lightly dust with icing sugar.

Potty Heligan Fruitcake

This special Heligan recipe is versatile enough to be used for any occasion. It's very easy to prepare and the end product is a wonderfully moist cake. As a novelty gift we bake this cake in flowerpots (see the Basic Bread Dough recipe p7), which we then decorate, for extra effect. Why not give this idea a try – the only limit is your imagination. (TB)

8 x 9cms/3½ins clay pots

For the cake
900g/2lb mixed fruit
340g/12oz self-raising flour
225g/8oz butter
170g/6oz dark brown sugar
55g/2oz chopped nuts
150mls/5fl oz milk
150mls/5fl oz water
2 tablespoons black treacle
2 tablespoons rum or brandy
1 teaspoon mixed spice
1 teaspoon cinnamon
4 eggs

For decoration
85g/3oz apricot jam
8 cherries
whole almonds

First season your pots as described on page 7.

Place the butter, water, milk, rum or brandy and dark brown sugar into a large saucepan and bring slowly to the boil. Add the mixed fruit and simmer for 10 minutes, then leave aside to cool. Once cooled, add the flour, spices, black treacle and eggs, taking care to mix thoroughly. Take your seasoned pots, grease them and place a circle of baking paper into the bottom of each one. Divide your cake mixture between the pots and bake in a pre-heated oven at 70°C/150°F/gas for 30–40 minutes. To test the cakes, insert a knife. If it is clean when removed, your cakes are ready. Leave to cool.

To decorate the tops of your cakes, heat the apricot jam for a couple of minutes, so that it is really bubbling and brush it over the cakes liberally. Then place a cherry in the centre of each one and arrange the almonds around the cherry to form a flower pattern. Glaze again with the apricot jam.

Pineapple Upside Down Cake

The pineapple pits at Heligan are quite unique – the only working example of this Victorian horticultural phenomenon, heated solely by copious amounts of rotting manure! (I really did not want to use these words around food, but without the many tons of this rich substance, there would be no fruit.) The man-hours involved in this method of growing pineapples suited the Victorians as labour was plentiful and cheap, but today, for the same cost, you could fly pineapples from the Caribbean, each with its own first class seat. However, the succulent sweet freshness of these rare home-grown fruits gives this somewhat well-used recipe a new lease of life. (PD)

For 8–10 portions

225g/8oz vanilla sugar
225g/8oz softened butter
285g/10oz self-raising flour
4 eggs
120mls/4fl oz golden syrup
1 small fresh pineapple
6 glacé cherries

Place the vanilla sugar and the butter in a large mixing bowl. With a wooden spoon beat until smooth and light in colour. Add half the flour along with 2 eggs and beat thoroughly. Finally, gradually add the remaining flour and eggs, alternating between the two and beating all the time. Grease and line with baking parchment a 25cms/10ins round cake tin (the type with a loose bottom). After peeling and removing the centre of your pineapple, slice into rings, and arrange around the bottom of your tin, with a glacé cherry in the centre of each slice. Pour over the golden syrup (I find heating the syrup in the microwave briefly helps). Spoon over the cake mixture and level with the back of a spoon. Bake in a preheated oven 180°C/350°F/gas 4 for 30–35 minutes or until when you insert a sharp knife the blade is removed clean. When cooked, leave in the tin and allow to cool for 30 minutes. While still warm run a knife around the sides of the cake before turning upside down onto a suitable serving plate. Give the bottom a few sharp taps and gently lift the tin. You should be left with only the base of the tin and the baking parchment stuck to the top, which can be peeled off easily. Allow to cool completely before cutting – alternatively serve hot with a generous amount of creamy smooth custard.

Farmhouse Fruit Cake

Fruit cake is always a versatile recipe to have. We use mixed spice in this version, but I can assure you that it's also very nice with cinnamon and some stewed apple thrown in. Of course, if you were to replace the mixed fruit with cherries, you would have a gorgeous cherry cake. Never be afraid to experiment; it's how a lot of good recipes come about, and it's mighty good fun eating all the cake as well! (TB)

For 8 portions

340g/12oz self-raising flour
225g/8oz caster sugar
225g/8oz margarine
340g/12oz mixed fruit
28g/1oz demerara sugar (for topping)
6 teaspoons mixed spice
4 eggs

Place the sugar and margarine into a food mixer and mix until light. Beat the eggs and add gradually, along with the flour, until all used. Finally mix in the spice and the fruit. Place into a greased and floured 2lb loaf tin, 25cms/10ins x 13cms/5ins x 6cms/2½ins deep and sprinkle generously with the demerara sugar. Bake in a pre-heated oven at 170°C/325°F/gas 3 for 40 minutes. Test by inserting a knife into the cake. If it comes out clean, the cake is ready.

Fiery Chocolate Fudge Cake

During the nineteenth century many Cornish miners went to Mexico in order to make their fortunes. The biggest mines were set up, managed and owned by a Cornishman who was so keen that his Cornish workers settle in that he introduced the pasty to the Mexican menu. Even to this day it is still one of the most readily available dishes when you visit the mining areas of Mexico. So, given this fact, there has to be a trade off, and what did they give us? Chilli and chocolate! At first this sounds like a practical joke cake, and perhaps the Mexicans did invent it for a laugh, but give it a go, make the cake and I promise you will be most pleasantly surprised. (TB)

For the sponge
340g/12oz self-raising flour
225g/8oz caster sugar
225g/8oz margarine
55g/2oz cocoa powder
4 eggs
1 small chopped chilli

For the fudge icing
225g/8oz icing sugar
55g/2oz butter
45mls/1½fl oz milk
2 tablespoons cocoa powder

For decoration
55g/2oz chocolate
6 chillies

Place the margarine and sugar into a food mixer and beat until pale and light, then add half of the flour and two eggs, taking care to mix well. Add the remaining flour and eggs, along with the cocoa powder and chilli, again mixing thoroughly. Grease and flour two 20.5cms/8ins round tins and divide the mixture between them. Bake in a pre-heated oven at 180°C/350°F/gas 4 for 30–40 minutes until the sponge springs back when pressed. Turn out and leave to cool on a wire rack.

Next make the fudge icing. Melt the butter. Place the icing sugar and cocoa powder into a mixer, add the milk and melted butter and beat until a soft spreadable icing has formed. If the icing is too thick just add a few more drops of milk until you reach the desired consistency.

Once the sponges are cool, sandwich them together with some of the icing. Then spread the rest of the icing over the top and sides of the cake. To decorate, dip the chillies into some melted chocolate and leave to set on some baking paper. Arrange on top of the cake.

Apricot Victoria Sandwich

Cakes are great! Everybody likes cakes. They bring happiness into everyone's lives. At Christmas, birthdays and weddings there's always a beautiful cake. Without our customers' undying love of cakes, our bakery at Heligan would not exist and neither would this book! So here is a traditional recipe with a slight twist your Granny will love. (PD)

For 6–8 portions

For the sponge
170g/6oz caster sugar
170g/6oz self-raising flour
170g/6oz softened butter
3 eggs
55g/2oz chopped dried apricots

For the filling
85g/3oz icing sugar
110g/4oz softened butter
A few drops of vanilla essence
85g/3oz apricot jam

Start with the sponge. In a large mixing bowl cream together the butter and sugar until light in colour. Beat the eggs and gradually mix into the butter, alternating between a little sifted flour and a splash of egg, until both are thoroughly combined in the mixture. Finally add the chopped apricots giving the mix a good stir. Butter and flour two 18cms/7ins round cake tins. Divide the mixture between the two and spread out evenly. Bake at 180°C/350°F/gas 4 for 15–20 minutes until golden, and the surface springs back when lightly pressed with the fingertips. Remove from the oven and cool a little, before turning onto a wire rack to cool completely.

To make butter cream, simply mix together the butter, icing sugar, a few drops of vanilla and beat vigorously until light in colour. Spread the top of one sponge with apricot jam and the bottom of the other with butter cream, sandwiching the two sponges together, place on a doily and using a sieve, lightly dust the top with icing sugar. Best served with a nice pot of Earl Grey tea.

I have discovered a strange phenomenon since coming to Cornwall some years ago; just try walking through Penzance on a busy lunchtime; there must be at least 10 bakers in the town, all a hive of activity. And outside each one there always seem to be several OAPs gazing lovingly at the display, causing an obstruction while literally 'window-shopping for buns'.

Bishop's Slice

A wonderfully easy little cake that always goes down well. However, this indulgent little treat does have one endearing quality that guarantees its success – it's named after me! (TB)

For 6–8 portions

For the pastry
225g/8oz plain flour
110g/4oz margarine
40mls/1½fl oz water

For the filling
225g/8oz self-raising flour
225g/8oz caster sugar
225g/8oz softened margarine
110g/4oz desiccated coconut
1 jar strawberry jam
4 eggs

Place the flour in a large mixing bowl, rub in the margarine and slowly add the water until a soft dough.

Keeping a little coconut aside for decoration, place the caster sugar and margarine into a food mixer and blend until pale, then add the flour, coconut and eggs, mixing thoroughly.

Roll the pastry out on a lightly floured table to fit a 20cm/8ins flan tin that has also been greased and floured. Place into the tin and trim the edges. Cover the bottom with the strawberry jam and then spread the filling evenly over the top. Sprinkle on the remaining coconut. Bake in a pre-heated oven at 150°C/300°F/gas 2 for 30–40 minutes until springy to the touch. Leave to cool before you slice.

Zesty Lemon Biscuits

This is a typical winter recipe. Not because of its ingredients, but purely because the act of cutting out individual biscuits and sandwiching them together with a lemon icing would be too time consuming in the summer months, when production is stepped up, with recipes involving 120 eggs, whole sacks of flour and 25lb/12kg sugar being the norm. We would be making many batches of this size every day just to keep up with demand. Taking time out to do dainty little things in the winter is a real treat and those busy days of August are forgotten for a brief moment. (PD)

For 12–15 biscuits

225g/8oz softened butter
110g/4oz caster sugar
225g/8oz plain flour
85g/3oz rice flour
3 unwaxed lemons
110g/4oz icing sugar

Place the butter and caster sugar in a food mixer and beat until pale in colour. Sift in the flour and rice flour, adding the zest of 3 lemons. Continue mixing until a smooth paste is formed, cling film and chill for 15 minutes. Roll out on a lightly floured table until 5mm/$\frac{1}{4}$in thick and with a cookie cutter cut as many as you can (this depends on the size of your cutter). Carefully move them onto a lightly buttered baking tray, return to the fridge for half an hour to relax the biscuit dough. Bake in a preheated oven 170°C/325°F/gas 3 for 15–20 minutes until light-golden in colour. Remove and allow to cool for 5 minutes before moving onto a wire rack to cool completely. When removed from the oven the texture will still be quite soft but the biscuits will crisp up as they cool down.

For the filling, sift the icing sugar gradually and add juice from the lemons, just enough to make the icing of a 'dropping' consistency. Spread some of the icing on the top of half the biscuits, placing the other biscuits on top to form a sandwich. Leave icing to firm up for half an hour before serving.

Rhubarb and Elderflower Roulade

Rhubarb, a herb originally grown in China and then Europe, was first imported at a high price in the early 1700s for its medicinal properties. Reputedly good for 'binding the belly, the staying of lasks and flux', and works wonders if you are suffering with 'swollen kernels'! Scientific uses aside... the sharpness of the rhubarb and the subtle floral flavour of the cream contrast perfectly and, when garnished with edible spring flowers, this looks superb. (PD)

For 6–8

For the compote
225g/8oz rhubarb
55g/2oz caster sugar
a splash of water

For the cream
290mls/10fl oz double cream
2–3 tablespoons elderflower cordial

For the sponge
225g/8oz self-raising flour
225g/8oz caster sugar
4 eggs
30g/1oz melted butter
12 primrose flowers
a dusting of icing sugar

First put the rhubarb with the sugar and just a splash of water in a saucepan, cover and cook gently until completely soft. Remove lid and cook until all excess liquid has reduced down, remove from heat and cool thoroughly. Now for the sponge: place the sugar and eggs in a food mixer and whisk for at least 10 minutes until light in colour, thick and frothy. Sift the flour and fold in with a metal spoon, then add the melted butter and fold in, taking care not to knock out all the air. Evenly spread the mixture out onto a greased and lined baking tray or Swiss roll tin. Bake in a preheated oven 220°C/425°F/gas 7 for 6–8 minutes until light-golden and the surface springs back when lightly pressed with the finger tips. Place the sponge (still on the greaseproof paper) onto a clean tea towel, sprinkle with caster sugar and roll up in the towel and allow to cool. Whip the cream until 'soft peaks' stage, adding elderflower cordial to taste and continue whipping until stiff peaks are formed. To assemble, gently unroll the sponge, remove the greaseproof before spreading the compote over the surface, followed by the elderflower cream. Carefully roll up and chill until you are ready to serve. To serve, cut into slices, dust with icing sugar and garnish with primroses.

Hazelnut Meringue with Strawberries

This dessert has featured at one of our now legendary Feast Nights here at Heligan. As a bit of a twist we piped the meringue to resemble a tree fern, but you can really do as you please. The fresh strawberries complement the meringue beautifully (as they do clotted cream – or should that be the other way around?) so give this one a go as it really is a true taste of summer. (TB)

For 6–8 portions

450g/1lb caster sugar
110g/4oz finely chopped hazelnuts
225g/8oz fresh strawberries
8 egg whites
whipping cream
8 sprigs fresh mint

Making sure that your bowl is perfectly clean, whisk the egg whites to a soft peak in a food mixer. Add the sugar and whisk for a further 2–3 minutes until firm peaks are formed. Gently fold in the hazelnuts. Using a plain nozzle, pipe the mixture onto a tray lined with baking paper, to a 20cms/8ins circle. Bake in a pre-heated oven at 100°C/200°F/gas ½ for 1½ – 2 hours to dry out the meringue. Leave to cool. Whip the cream and pipe onto the meringue base, decorating with the fresh strawberries and a sprinkling of chopped hazelnuts. Top off with some fresh mint leaves.

Rose Petal and Peach Cheesecake

If there is one flavour that sums up the taste of Heligan it must be our fresh home-grown peaches. Their season is very short and so far only Feast Night customers have been lucky enough to taste them. This recipe is the only one in this book not to have been served at Heligan. I developed this dessert especially for this book, and I am very pleased with it. I can't wait to offer it to our customers this summer. (PD)

For 6–8 portions

1 small packet digestive biscuits
55g/2oz butter
340g/12oz cream cheese
290mls/10fl oz whipping cream
55g/2oz caster sugar
150mls/5fl oz of rosewater
3 fresh ripe peaches
a handful of rose petals

Grease and line the bottom of a 25cms/10ins cake tin (the sort with a loose bottom) and crush all the biscuits in a bowl, using the end of a rolling pin. Melt the butter in a pan and add the biscuit crumbs, mix thoroughly before tipping into the cake tin, spreading out and patting down firm with the back of a spoon. Then chill in the fridge for at least half an hour. Dissolve the sugar in the rosewater and stir into the cream cheese, mixing until smooth. Whip the cream, fold into the cheese mixture, and give a final whisk until stiff peaks are formed. Spoon this onto the biscuit base, smooth out flat and return to the fridge for at least 2 hours, before carefully removing from the tin (to do this remove the outer rim of the tin and slide off the base onto a suitable serving plate). Remove the skin and stones from the peaches, cut into segments and arrange these on top of your cheesecake in a circular pattern. Finally, just before serving, sprinkle a handful of rose petals over the top. These are edible and something your guests won't see used everyday.

Raspberry Fool with Cat's Tongues

Before you phone your local butcher and give him a fright, cat's tongues or 'langues de chat' are delicious little piped biscuits like shortbread, only much finer and very light. These can accompany many desserts and go perfectly with these summery fools, served in wine glasses and topped with an overgenerous amount of fresh raspberries and whipped cream. (PD)

For 6–8

For the biscuits
100g/3½ oz plain flour
100g/3½ oz softened butter
100g/3½ oz caster sugar
3 egg whites

For the fool
290mls/10fl oz cold cooked custard – made from custard powder
350mls/12fl oz whipping cream
450g/1lb fresh raspberries
55g/2oz icing sugar
6–8 sprigs mint

First make the biscuits. Place the butter and sugar in a mixing bowl, beating until fluffy and pale in colour. Whisk the egg-whites until quite frothy but not stiff and carefully fold into the butter and sugar, before folding in the sifted flour, using a metal spoon. Grease and line a baking sheet, then using a piping bag with a plain nozzle, pipe into fingers, 5cms/2ins long. Bake in a preheated oven 200°C/400°F/gas 6 for 5–8 minutes until light-golden in the centre and a little darker at the edges. Allow to cool before removing with a palette knife.

Now on to the fool: whip the cream until stiff, crush 285g/10oz of the raspberries, mixing in the icing sugar until dissolved. Fold together the custard and crushed fruit, then fold in the cream, keeping back enough to pipe 6–8 rosettes. Spoon the mixture into tall wine glasses leaving a gap at the top to fill with the remaining raspberries. These are best bruised a little, not crushed, just enough to make the fruit bleed slightly. On top of this pipe a rosette of cream and place a sprig of mint. Chill for at least an hour and serve with cat's tongues on the side.

Summer Pudding

The quintessentially English summer dessert. All those summer berries, a glass of Pimm's on the side, a dollop of cream on the top, what could be better? Just imagine – having trugs of plump home-grown soft fruits brought to your kitchen door by a dedicated team of skilled gardeners – I don't need to imagine; after all, I am in chef's heaven! I apologise for this smugness and now must get on with the recipe...summer puddings can be made with many varieties of fruit, using different blends, with different fruits being the prominent character, even adding a dash of Cassis or Kirsch – the possibilities are endless. Just experiment and have fun. (PD)

For 6

900g/2lb soft fruits (i.e. redcurrants, blackcurrants, gooseberries, blackberries, myrtles, strawberries, raspberries)
2 tablespoons hot water
170g/6oz caster sugar
8–10 slices white bread

Take a large saucepan and add the hot water, sugar, redcurrants, blackcurrants, myrtles and blackberries. Heat gently for 5 minutes until just soft and remove from the heat before adding the strawberries and raspberries. Drain off most of the liquid into a jug, dip the slices of bread into this juice and use these to line a pudding basin. Pour in the cooked fruit and place a circle of bread on the top. Cool in a fridge overnight, with a plate and heavy weight on the top e.g. a can of beans. Return the remaining juice to the pan and simmer until reduced by half; leave in a fridge overnight. To serve, remove the plate and weight before carefully turning out into a suitable serving plate (my tip for doing this is to first put the serving plate on top of the basin before turning both over and giving a quick sharp shake). Drizzle with the reduced fruit juice and serve with thick double cream.

Apple Charlotte with Honey and Cinnamon Yoghurt

Apples conjure up many images: toffee apples, an apple a day keeps the doctor away, bobbing for apples, cider-madness... and of course the apple in the Garden of Eden. My first memory of apples was also as an object of temptation – unable to resist I was soon climbing Mr Brown's apple tree and scrumping his prize Cox's Pippins. This activity was much frowned upon. Undeterred, scrumping is still something I do (although now called foraging) and apples are replaced with wild mushrooms, ramsons, samphire and hedgerow fruits. Apple Charlotte is as tempting as apples can get. Perfect on a blustery autumn evening. (PD)

For 6

8 slices granary bread
110g/4oz caster sugar
55g/2oz fresh breadcrumbs
450g/1lb peeled and cored Bramley apples
170g/6oz butter
2 teaspoons ground cinnamon
6 cloves
350mls/12fl oz thick Greek style yoghurt
1 tablespoon clear honey

Butter all the slices of bread completely from edge to edge. Take a deep baking dish and line with slices of bread and butter – butter side down. Cut the remaining slices into quarters diagonally and set aside. Melt a large knob of butter in a saucepan, adding the apples, cloves, 85g/3oz caster sugar, and 1 teaspoon of ground cinnamon. Cook until just starting to soften, stir in the breadcrumbs and remove from heat. Turn the mixture into the bread-lined dish, smooth out flat and arrange the bread triangles to cover the top – butter side up. Melt the remaining butter and drizzle over, making sure some goes down the sides to soak into the bread. Sprinkle with the remaining caster sugar and bake in a preheated oven 180°C/350°F/gas 4 for 30–40 minutes until crisp and golden and the bread underneath has fried in the melted butter. Serve hot with honey and cinnamon yoghurt. For this, simply mix together in advance the honey, yoghurt and 1 teaspoon of cinnamon and refrigerate until needed. Traditionally this dessert is made in small individual portions cooked in a dariole mould – this is done in just the same way, only the cooking time is reduced a little.

Citrus House Soufflé (cold)

I first stumbled into the citrus house one hot summer's day purely by accident. I ventured into the gardens with another chef, Austin, intent on plundering some very fine herbs, and grazing on strawberries as we went. Our picking was soon interrupted by a large swarm of bees entering the walled garden, darkening the sky and filling the air with a menacing drone. The level-headed Austin reassured the public, instructing them not to panic. Within a minute the bees had gone – Austin turned to me to find I had sprinted 100 yards and locked myself inside what I discovered to be the citrus house, leaving only a chef's hat where I had once stood! (PD)

For 6

1 lime
1 lemon
1 orange
170g/6oz caster sugar
350mls/12½ oz double cream
3 large eggs*
15g/fioz leaf gelatine
6 sprigs basil

Soak the gelatine in cold water for 10 minutes. Separate the eggs, putting the yolks, sugar and the juice and zest of the lemon, lime and half the orange into a heatproof bowl. Whisk this over a pan of hot water until the mixture thickens and turns light in colour. Squeeze the water from the leaf gelatine and stir it into the mixture until dissolved. Remove from the heat. Whip the egg whites until stiff and separately whip the cream until soft peaks are formed. Using a metal spoon, gently fold the cream into the citrus mixture followed by the egg whites (a cutting and lifting action avoids knocking out all the air). When thoroughly blended, spoon the mixture into 6 tall wine glasses and chill for at least 2 hours before piping a cream rosette on each. Garnish with a twist of orange and a sprig of basil.

*As this dish contains raw eggs please ensure they are very fresh. It is well worth noting that eggs with a lion-mark come from chickens vaccinated against salmonella. I would recommend only using these eggs for this recipe.

This recipe uses a selection of citrus fruits and is based on the classic soufflé Milanaise.

Bitter Chocolate Syllabub with Hazelnut Praline

No matter what delights the Heligan gardeners produce for us: pineapples, peaches, many summer berries and citrus fruits, there are some of us who do not want a delicious fruity dessert, fresh and full of the taste of summer. There is a little voice inside us that seems to cry out 'Chocolate!' Every menu all over the world must provide something for the chocaholic contingency. There is a little bit of the chocaholic in all of us and sooner or later you are going to give into temptation; with me, it's sooner rather than later. So here is my indulgently rich chocolate syllabub. (PD)

For 6

For the syllabub
425mls/15fl oz double cream
1 tablespoon sunflower oil
2 tablespoons dry sherry
225g/8oz dark chocolate (the higher the cocoa percentage the better)
2 teaspoons cocoa powder
30g/1oz icing sugar

For the praline
110g/4oz caster sugar
85g/3oz chopped hazelnuts

Begin by making the praline. In a good saucepan (stainless steel is fine, but copper is best) place the caster sugar in the pan and heat over a moderate flame (this may seem crazy, but trust me it works) after a few minutes caramel will appear around the edges. Do not stir but gently shake, keep going until all the sugar has melted. Stir in the nuts and remove from heat. Immediately pour onto baking parchment, which in turn is on a metal tray – allow to cool completely. I find giving the saucepan to somebody else to wash works best!

Melt the chocolate over a pan of simmering water (but not touching the water). Meanwhile, whip the cream until soft peaks are formed, remove and save a quarter of this for use later. To the remaining cream add the icing sugar, cocoa and sherry, and stir in well. When the chocolate has melted pour in the sunflower oil and give it a good stir. Then add the chocolate to the cream, briskly folding in until even in colour. Spoon into glasses, followed by the cream you put aside spread evenly over the top. Take your now rock hard praline and crush with a rolling pin. Sprinkle this over the top and serve. This is a very rich dessert and best served after a light meal (maybe a little grilled fish rather than a 2lb steak and kidney pudding!).

Hot Cross Buns

For most people the humble hot cross bun signals that once again, Easter is upon us, Bank Holidays come thick and fast and the prospect of stuffing chocolate eggs until we burst is only days away. I should be so lucky! These tasty little treats signal the start of our summer season, which means incredibly early starts and shifts that seemingly go on for days! How I just love this traditional Easter fare! (TB)

For 8–10 buns

For the buns
450g/1lb strong white flour
110g/4oz sultanas
55g/2oz currants
55g/2oz caster sugar
55g/2oz softened butter
30g/1oz fresh yeast
150mls/5fl oz warm water
150mls/5fl oz milk
4 teaspoons mixed spice
1 teaspoon caster sugar
$\frac{1}{2}$ teaspoon salt
1 egg

For the crosses
55g/2oz plain flour
55mls/2fl oz water

For the glaze
55g/2oz caster sugar
55mls/2fl oz water

Prepare the yeast liquid by mixing the yeast with one teaspoon of caster sugar, the milk and warm water. Place the strong white flour, salt, mixed spice, caster sugar and fruit into a large mixing bowl. Rub in the softened butter, then add the egg. Slowly introduce the yeast liquid (you may not need it all) and mix until a soft dough is formed. Cover this with a damp cloth and leave to prove until doubled in size. Turn out onto a lightly floured table and knead gently for a few minutes. Divide into balls and place on a greased and floured baking tray. Leave in a warm place until doubled in size. To make the crosses, blend your flour and water to a paste and pipe onto the top of the risen buns. Bake in a pre-heated oven at 180°C/350°F/gas 4 for 15 minutes or until lightly browned. For the glaze, gently boil the sugar and water together and brush onto the buns while they are still hot. Leave to cool on a wire rack and serve with lashings of real butter.

Simnel Cake

Traditionally served at Easter, the decoration of twelve balls is said to represent the apostles. Some, who feel strongly enough, serve the cake with only eleven balls, the one missing representing Judas. Whichever you choose to do, eleven or twelve apostles, you will have a substantial and incredibly tasty cake that you may well find yourself making all year round. (TB)

Makes 10–12 portions

170g/6oz softened butter
170g/6oz dark brown sugar
255g/9oz self-raising flour
450g/1lb currants
110g/4oz sultanas
170g/6oz raisins
55g/2oz cherries
2 tablespoons milk
1 teaspoon mixed spice
1 teaspoon cinnamon
3 eggs
450g/1lb marzipan
55g/2oz apricot jam

Beat the eggs, then place the sugar and butter into a mixer and beat for 1 minute. Add half of the flour and half of the egg and beat together. Mix in the remaining flour and egg and the spices, then all the fruit and milk, taking care to mix thoroughly. Roll out half of the marzipan and cut to a circle of 20cms/8 ins. It is a good idea to use your cake tin as a template for this circle to ensure the correct size. Take your cake tin, line with baking paper and pour half of the cake mix into it. Level out the mixture and place the marzipan circle over the top. Pour on the remaining cake mixture and smooth out evenly. Bake in a pre-heated oven at 140°C/275°F/gas 1 for 2–2½ hours. The cake is ready when a skewer can be removed clean from the cake. Leave to cool and then turn out.

Boil the apricot jam and spread over the top of the cake. Take three quarters of the marzipan and roll to a circle big enough to cover the top. Take the last of the marzipan and roll into twelve (or eleven) balls and place in a ring on top of the cake. You can use a little water to stick them on if needed. As further decoration, I then carefully make a criss-cross pattern in the centre with a sharp knife and gently brown the cake under the grill for a few seconds. If you decide to do this be very careful as the marzipan burns very easily.

Tunis Cake

This delicate sponge cake is traditionally served at Christmas and is one of my favourites because, during the winter, I have more time and like to decorate it with perfect little marzipan fruits. As with some other recipes, good quality chocolate is essential. (TB)

Makes 10–12 portions

For the cake
225g/8oz self-raising flour
170g/6oz softened butter
170g/6oz caster sugar
110g/4oz ground almonds
1 lemon (juice and grated rind)
3 eggs

For the topping
plenty of good quality chocolate
6 marzipan fruits (see recipe on opposite page)

First make the cake. Place the butter and sugar into a food mixer and beat until pale. Add the eggs, flour, lemon juice, lemon rind and ground almonds, mixing thoroughly. Place the mixture into a 20cms/8ins greased and floured tin and bake in a pre-heated oven at 150°C /300°F/gas 2 for 1 hour or until springy in the middle when pressed. Leave on a wire rack to cool.

To decorate the cake, wrap some greaseproof paper around the sides of the cake, standing proud of the top, secure this with a piece of string. This forms a well into which you can pour the melted chocolate. Remove the greaseproof and you'll find that the chocolate shouldn't have run down the sides. Ideally, you should have one centimetre of chocolate – yes really! Leave to set and place the marzipan fruits on the top to finish.

Marzipan Fruits and Handmade Chocolates

These are very easy to create and make a great gift idea for Christmas. They are also used as decoration for our Tunis (opp) and Easter Simnel (p47) cakes, the recipes for which you will find in this book. Here, too, are just a few ideas for making some very easy chocolates. During the busy summer months, when I've made tray after tray of flapjacks and shortbread, I dream of the wintertime when I can fiddle around making chocolates and marzipan fruits. (TB)

Marzipan Fruits

Oranges
Colour some marzipan with a little orange food colouring, then divide into small balls about 2cms/1in in diameter. Take the balls one at a time and gently roll them over the fine side of a grater to give the pitted appearance. Finally insert a clove into the top of each orange.

Bananas
Colour some marzipan with yellow colouring (or turmeric, which was Paul's tip to me when I ran out of colouring). Divide and shape into small bananas, inserting a clove in the end of each one to resemble the stalk.

Strawberries
Colour your marzipan to a deep pink, divide and roll into balls. Gently shape each to resemble a strawberry, roll in caster sugar and use a small stick of angelica as a stalk.

Lemons
Colour some marzipan yellow, divide and roll into balls. Gently shape to resemble a lemon then roll in caster sugar.

Chocolates

Makes 20–30

85g/3oz milk chocolate
85g/3oz dark chocolate
85g/3oz white chocolate
(any baking chocolate is fine)
petits fours cases

Melt your chocolates separately, either in glass bowls over simmering water or in plastic jugs in the microwave (carefully!). Arrange your petits fours cases into trays and decide on what ingredients you are going to add for flavour (mint or orange), texture (small or chopped nuts) or colour (simply layering the assorted chocolates).

As a suggestion why not try mint oil with 25g/1oz caster sugar for mint crisps or perhaps chopped apricots. Tangerine and lavender oils make lovely chocolates. Just use your imagination. Once set, the chocolates will keep for a couple of weeks in a container. Do not store in the fridge.

Coconut Ice

At Heligan Christmas is a time for doing things we would never have time for in the summer. The crowds have gone; the autumn harvest and all the preserving, pickling and drying that goes with it has finished. In the kitchen we have the time to start using more elaborate recipes. After feeding 4,000 per day during the summer months this is quite a welcome break. It is at this time Christmas cakes, puddings, home-made chocolates and sweetmeats are all produced. Along with these, coconut ice is made from a very simple recipe. But where did I get this recipe? Escoffier? Huber? Cesarani? No, Blue Peter circa 1978! Well it works every time and makes a great gift 'for your mother or an elderly aunt', according to the Blue Peter presenter! (PD)

For 40–60 pieces

1 x 397g tin of condensed milk
450g/1lb icing sugar
450g/1lb desiccated coconut
a few drops of pink food colouring

This could not be simpler. A food mixer is a good idea if you are doing more than one batch. Start by mixing together the icing sugar, coconut and condensed milk. When thoroughly mixed remove half and spread out over one half of a lined baking tray and press down with the back of a spoon. Add the pink colouring to the remaining mixture and stir in until an even colour. Spread the pink mixture over the other half of the tray, again pressing down with the back of a spoon. Leave to set in a cool place (not the fridge) for at least 2 hours before cutting into little squares. Store in an airtight jar or tin.

Figgy Pudding

Not content with making just any old Christmas pudding, I decided to do a little research. Influenced by the Victorian feel of the gardens, old 19th century recipes were the order of the day. I found Mrs Beeton particularly inspiring – the Victorians loved their steamed suet puddings. We decided to make traditional Christmas pudding, as well as figgy pudding with rum and apricot pudding with brandy, all loosely based on Mrs. Beeton's originals. Some of her other great puddings were: Delhi pudding, Canary pudding and bone marrow dumplings! (PD)

For one 2 pint pudding

450g/1lb chopped dried figs
55g/2oz sultanas
170g/6oz fresh breadcrumbs
140g/5oz vegetable suet
85g/3oz self-raising flour
85g/3oz muscovado sugar
3 eggs
2 tablespoons rum
1 lemon
1 orange
1 teaspoon ground cinnamon
2 teaspoons mixed spice
a little milk

Juice and zest the orange and lemon into a large mixing bowl, add all the ingredients except the milk, mix thoroughly until completely blended. If the mixture is a little dry then add a splash of milk (this will depend on how large the orange and lemon were to start with and how generous you were with the rum). Turn the mixture into a well-buttered 2 pint pudding basin, cover with a circle of greaseproof paper with tinfoil on top tying a piece of string around the rim. Steam the pudding for approximately 3 hours over boiling water, or place in a roasting tray half filled with boiling water and cook in a low oven preheated to 130°C/250°F/gas 1 for 2 hours. Serve with custard, brandy butter or fresh cream.

Late one night I even had some accompanied by Beef Wellington and Sauce Porto; but then I had been in a hot kitchen for 15 hours!

As a font of all knowledge Mrs Beeton also goes on to advise on the good eating of 'larks' and the not so good eating of 'guinea pigs'. She also discovered 'an excellent substitute for milk or cream in tea or coffee…just allow 1 raw egg for every cup…'

Christmas Cake

These days most of us decorate our Christmas cakes with marzipan and royal icing and this is viewed as traditional. However many countries use just marzipan or glazed fruits as topping, and to say that the latter looks truly mouth-watering is an understatement. We write our festive greeting in Cornish (Nadelek Lowen). Of course, if you wanted to be really alternative, you could always use a set of fairy lights to add that extra sparkle! (TB)

Makes 10–12 portions

900g/2lb mixed fruit
340g/12oz self-raising flour
225g/8oz butter
170g/6oz dark brown sugar
110g/4oz cherries (halved)
55g/2oz chopped nuts
150mls/5fl oz milk
150mls/5fl oz water
2 tablespoons black treacle
2 tablespoons rum or brandy
2 teaspoons mixed spice
1 teaspoon cinnamon
1 teaspoon grated nutmeg
4 eggs

Place the butter, milk, water, rum/brandy and dark brown sugar into a large saucepan and slowly bring to the boil. Add the mixed fruit and cherries and simmer gently for 10 minutes. Leave to cool. Once cooled add the flour, spices, eggs, black treacle and chopped nuts, mixing thoroughly. Line a 18cms/7–8ins tin with baking paper and pour in mixture. Bake in a pre-heated oven 70°C/150°F/gas ½ for 1–1½ hours. To test the cake, insert a knife. If it is clean when removed, your cake is ready.

Special Tip
When I bake this cake, I put a tin of water into the bottom of the oven as it gives the cake more moisture

Christmas Meringue with Marsala Sabayon

Here is a great alternative to mince pies, served with a light frothy Marsala sabayon. This sounds impressive but it is in fact very easy to make. This recipe is of Italian origin, known as Zabaglione alla Marsala, served as a sort of adult milk shake. Superb on its own but when used as a sauce it complements many desserts. I first cooked this meringue in a restaurant 20 years ago. There, dowsed with brandy, we would send them out with flames leaping from the top. They were always well received – waiters' singed eyebrows notwithstanding! (PD)

For 6–8 portions

For the pastry
340g/12oz plain flour
85g/3oz caster sugar
200g/7oz softened butter
1 egg

For the filling
450g/1lb mincemeat
6 egg whites
340g/12oz caster sugar

For the sabayon
6 egg yolks
170g/6oz caster sugar
150mls/5fl oz Marsala

Place all pastry ingredients in a food mixer on the lowest speed, mix until malleable, smooth and even textured. Wrap in cling film and chill for one hour. Lightly grease a 25cms/10ins quiche dish and roll out the pastry on a floured table. Carefully line the dish with pastry and trim around the edges with a small knife, before evenly spreading the mincemeat over the pastry base. Bake in a preheated oven 180°C/350°F/gas 4 for 20–25 minutes. Remove and set aside. Whisk the egg whites in a food mixer along with 170g/6oz caster sugar. When stiff peaks are formed add the remaining 170g/6oz sugar and whisk for a further minute. Take a piping bag with a star nozzle and pipe large rosettes covering the entire surface until all the meringue has been used. Place in a preheated oven 200°C/400°F/gas 6 until golden brown (this can happen quite fast). Remove, cut and serve with a sabayon sauce. For this, simply whisk the egg yolks and the sugar in a bowl until almost white in colour, then mix in the Marsala. Place the bowl over a pan of simmering water, whisk until frothy and four times its volume. Serve immediately.

Partners in Pabulum

Tina Bishop
Baker

Tina was 'born and bred' in Cornwall, and has been in bakery and confectionary for seventeen years to date. Having trained at Plymouth College of Further Education, she went on to open her own bakery in Truro, where she proved her unrivalled ability to produce the most spectacular celebration cakes.

She started work at the Lost Gardens of Heligan in 1999 and has found a job that she genuinely loves. Most enjoyable of all, for Tina, is the opportunity that she gets to express her creative flair and come up with new lines for the Heligan bakery. Couple this with her ability to produce cakes at an amazing rate and you really do have the perfect recipe for success.

Included here are a few of Tina's favourite and most popular recipes that we can only recommend (even insist!) that you try first hand. Your taste buds will be eternally grateful!

Paul says of Tina: A skilful and prolific baker, capable of producing phenomenal amounts, while maintaining high standards of culinary excellence at all times.

Paul Drye
Head Chef and Catering Manager

After twenty years as a Chef, including holding the position of Head Chef at a number of excellent restaurants, and then Catering Manager for a large corporate catering management company, Paul then made a life-changing decision to leave the rat-race in 1997, which led him to a place he calls 'chef's heaven' – otherwise known as the Lost Gardens of Heligan.

His new lifestyle involved cooking with the best home grown fruit, vegetables and herbs, locally caught fish, organically reared meats and the finest Cornish ingredients – 'Real food for Real People'. The Friday Feast Nights at Heligan are a good opportunity to experience this philosophy in practice.

Wild food is a particular passion of his. Regular forays in the countryside with his wife Angela and their bull terrier, Ellie, lead them to a variety of mushrooms, wild herbs, and hedgerow fruits, along with lazy days fishing off the rocks – it seems if you know where to look there is such a thing as a 'free lunch'!

Paul is Catering Manager as well as Head Chef, but is still a hands-on chef for high days and holidays and of course Feast Nights.

Tina says of Paul: His ability to create the most amazing dishes from just about any ingredients is a testimony to the outstanding culinary skills that Paul naturally possesses.

Postscript

A Day in the Life of a Heligan Chef

The first impression when reading this book is of chefs working with wonderful ingredients in beautiful surroundings, cooking good food for appreciative customers and having a good laugh, should the opportunity arise. This image of 'chef's heaven', although slightly rose tinted, is quite true. What I have neglected to mention is just how much hard work it is. Let's look at a typical summers' day – a Tuesday in August is as good as it gets...

At 8am Heligan is a magical place but appreciated for a brief moment as I walk to the kitchen. I'm not the first in - baking has been going on for hours and you take in calories just by breathing in. I flick on the ovens and start to plan the lunch menu. With produce arriving from the gardens daily, we like to be spontaneous rather than plan menus weeks ahead. The second chef arrives and takes over the lunch preparation. We have decided to go for carrot, orange and coriander soup (80 pints should do), aubergines stuffed with cous cous, sun dried tomatoes and basil, and rainbow trout baked with bulb fennel, butter and almonds.

I move on to the food for the evening's Feast Night. I had worked on this menu all the previous day, getting the basics done, and now it's just a case of bringing it all together. Cutting garnishes, slicing terrines

terrines, rolling fillets of brill in fresh herbs, piping chocolate filigree, spinning sugar and a hundred and one other things. It all gets done, and just before service I am pacing up and down impatiently, waiting for the first of a hundred diners to arrive. I am psyched up because there are just two of us in the kitchen and 300 plated and garnished dishes to go out in the next two hours – every one to look perfect. Tonight the service goes well, apart from the lady who asked for ice cream – the two desserts I made obviously weren't good enough! I hand-picked those lemons and limes from our own trees in the citrus house, the eggs and cream were from local farmers, while the other dessert was made from the finest organic dark chocolate, garnished with chocolate filigree that almost defied gravity; but ice cream she wanted!

Once the devastation in the kitchen is cleared away, the staff sit down for a well-earned bite. We talk about the day's events, how well the evening went and even laugh about the ice cream lady – before I finally leave for home around midnight. It's hard work in 'chef's heaven'!

Paul Drye (Head Chef and Catering Manager)